'The Twentieth Century h̶ the bloodiest in human history ...Some hundred million people have been killed in conflict.'

Professor Robert O'Neill

Founders

Peel Holdings plc

European Regional Development Fund

Trafford Metropolitan Borough Council

North West Development Agency

English Partnerships

The Trustees of the Imperial War Museum

Supporters

The Zochonis Charitable Trust

The Duchy of Lancaster Benevolent Fund

Stoller Charitable Trust

The Weston Family

European Social Fund

Learning and Skills Council Greater Manchester

Salford College

The Rank Foundation

The Lloyds TSB Foundation for England and Wales

The Trusthouse Charitable Foundation

Rolls-Royce plc

Department for Culture, Media and Sport

Bridge Insurance Brokers (Manchester) Ltd

The Barker Foundation

The Nationwide Foundation

Wilde + Spieth GmbH & co

Contributors

Architect **Studio Daniel Libeskind**

Exhibition Design **Real Studios Ltd**

Audio-Visual Design **Event Communications Ltd**

Big Picture Producers **Media Projects (Why War?)**

English and Co Ltd (Weapons and War, and Children and War)

Photography **Len Grant Photography**

Phil Sayer

Mark Follon

Michael Spencer-Jones

Owerka Lyle\Gamma

Guidebook design **SMITH**

Corporate ID **Agenda Associates**

Printed by **Balding+Mansell**

4\The Story of Imperial War Museum North

Daniel Libeskind, architect of Imperial War Museum North, told me once that this project was extremely challenging, not least because it contains three of the most difficult words in the English language: 'imperial', 'war' and 'museum'. He has risen to the challenge, however, and the architecture eloquently conveys the world-wide consequences of war.

The Imperial War Museum was created in 1917 because people wanted to record the huge contribution everyone had made in the First World War, at home and in the front line, by all the countries of the Empire. It was conceived as a people's museum, exploring differing experiences of war and the impact of war on people's lives. Committees gathered together an enormous range of material which laid the foundations for our huge collections spanning art, film, photographs, sound recordings, objects and documents. The scope of the Museum has changed over the years. It now encompasses all wars in which Commonwealth forces have been involved right up to the present day, including the Falklands, the Gulf War and wars in the former Yugoslavia.

When the Imperial War Museum opened in 1920, many people hoped that the First World War was the war to end all wars. Today, as this new branch opens, few people believe that we are likely to eliminate war in the foreseeable future. However, not all international tensions inevitably lead to war. People and public perceptions can influence decisions, and knowledge and understanding allow informed debate. By setting up Imperial War Museum North we hope that new audiences in a region ill-served by our existing branches will be enabled to delve into our remarkable collections, learn about their history and develop a deeper understanding of why wars occur.

Robert Crawford
Director-General, Imperial War Museum

War is extreme. People are pushed to their limits, which results in killing and devastation but also inspires exceptional courage and heroism. The Museum's collections reflect people's varied experience of war. Our challenge was to create a museum that put learning right at the centre, allowing visitors to discover the power of the collections and stimulating them to find out more about their history and its relevance today.

We developed an exhibitions and learning strategy that drew on the strength of the architecture, the collections and the way people learn. The **Big Picture** uses the dramatic interior space to encourage visitors to engage directly with the collections of sound, photographs and art. Whereas these shows deal with major thought-provoking issues, the **TimeStacks** give people the chance to select specific objects at the touch of a button. The **Timeline** puts people's experiences into a chronological framework whilst the exhibition **Silos** explore themes in greater detail. Our layered approach to learning enables people to absorb information on different levels.

Daniel Libeskind's architecture signals a museum with a difference. We have worked to integrate the exhibitions and the architecture, to create a unique place where you will see familiar things in a new light, and will want to come back again to explore different perspectives on history.

Vivienne Bennett
Project Director, Imperial War Museum North

5\Welcome

Museums are all about the interaction between people: being able to share experiences, reflect on aspects of history and handle or study objects. We have worked closely with community groups in developing the Museum and have established an active volunteer programme. This has ensured that a wide variety of people have been able to contribute to the venture from the start. We offer an extensive range of learning opportunities and events to create a vibrant social and educational hub where people can explore their history in a welcoming and inclusive environment. Here, in the Museum, everyone can learn from each other – different generations, different cultures, different backgrounds and perspectives.

Having seen our world shattered through the wars of the twentieth century, the question is whether we can rebuild something spectacular out of the pieces. We look forward to hearing your views and sharing your experiences.

Jim Forrester Director, Imperial War Museum North

6\Big Picture

The **Big Picture** exposes issues that lie at the heart of all wars and conflicts. Deliberately thought-provoking, they encourage debate and discussion about strong, and often controversial, subjects. The shows envelop the main exhibition space, surrounding visitors in a constantly changing environment of images and sound. The **Big Picture** is a new and experimental way to see and hear the Museum's outstanding collection of photographs, art and sound. Each show is a unique audio-visual experience.

The Museum commissioned independent production companies to create the first three shows. They were asked to draw upon the Museum's vast archives and to present a variety of views, which are not necessarily those of the Museum. In the shows people talk frankly about their experiences which are often moving and powerful.

7\Why War?

Why do wars happen? This is often the first question that people ask, yet there is rarely a simple answer.

In **Why War?** children, academics, a journalist, a soldier and a psychologist talk about the causes of some of the major wars in the last century. They also discuss the possible causes of future wars and how they might be prevented.

'Why do we have wars?'
Manchester schoolchild

'Peace is the absence of war. You have to actively promote peace to avoid war'
Kate Adie

8\Weapons of War

War has led to the development of increasingly sophisticated weapons such as poison gas and the atom bomb, and the refinement of existing weapons including the bayonet and the rifle. We now have an unprecedented number of ways of injuring and killing each other. **Weapons of War** looks behind the hardware to discover people's experiences of developing weapons in the laboratory and factory through to using them in the front line. The show contains powerful testimonies from people who have seen at first hand the consequences of our ingenuity for killing, including what it was like to be a victim of these weapons.

'Where before there had been a city now you couldn't see anything except this black boiling barrel of tar'

Colonel Paul Tibbets, pilot of the United States B-29 bomber *Enola Gay*, which dropped an atom bomb on the Japanese city of Hiroshima in 1945.

'Marvellous. Nobody can get me in here'

Unknown British soldier describing his feelings upon joining a tank crew.

9\Children and War

How do children see war? In this show children from Britain and around the world discuss their feelings about war. Some describe the excitement and trauma of being evacuated from their homes during the Second World War. Others describe being forced to flee their countries as refugees and their impressions of arriving in strange new lands. Child soldiers speak frankly about being in the front line. Children also talk about how they have survived war and their hopes for the future.

'When Hitler came it became very difficult for us. The children we played with spat on us'
Unknown German Jewish *Kindertransport* child refugee.

'I still have a war way of thinking. If I see a falling star I think it's a tracer'
Edin Hamzic, former Bosnian child soldier.

10\Timeline

The **Timeline** forms the backbone of the displays, giving an overall picture of how, when and why wars have been fought over the last hundred years, and the effect of those wars on people's lives.

The **Timeline** not only charts the changing balance of power in the world, it also focuses on the personal stories of leaders, soldiers in the front line and civilians at home. It shows how people have altered the course of history, whether as a famous political figure or as an unknown soldier.

Visitors can explore the sequence of events through objects, photographs, film and documents, and engage on different levels. They can make the connection between events, see emerging patterns and relate them to their own knowledge and experience. People may not agree with the choice of events, or their interpretation, but history is about argument and debate and the **Timeline** will undoubtedly stimulate discussion.

1900-1914
A New Century

Europe enjoys peace and prosperity.
It dominates the world but its grip is weakening.
The balance of power is changing.
Old empires are decaying. New powers are emerging.
Ambition, rivalry and fear force up spending on armies
and navies.
Former enemies become partners and two opposing
alliances form.
On the horizon, war threatens.

1914-1918
First World War

In 1914 war sweeps across Europe.
People from around the world are drawn in.
Eight million die in battle; thirteen million civilians
also die.
Shortages, air raids and increasing state control bring
the war home to everyone.
Hunger and defeat spark widespread revolt.
**The scale of suffering changes people's view of war
forever.**

1919-1939
Between the Wars

People begin to rebuild their lives.
In Germany, there is resentment over the terms of the
peace treaty.
Leaders talk and try to ban war.
Worldwide economic depression brings mass
unemployment and poverty.
Communism and fascism flourish by promising solutions.
In Europe dictators are on the march. In Asia, Japan sets
out to conquer.
World peace hangs by a thread.

1939-1945
The Second World War

Global conflict brings mass death and destruction.
55 million die on battlefields, in death camps,
in their homes.
Millions more become refugees.
Cities, towns and countryside are devastated.
Societies are shattered and nations smashed.
The impact of this war is total.

1946-1990
Cold War

From the ruins of war, two superpowers rise.
The United States and the Soviet Union dominate
the world.
Fearful and suspicious, they spy on one another.
Each builds up enough nuclear weapons to kill everyone.
Avoiding head-on conflict, they shadow-box in wars
around the world.
**Then, with little warning, the Soviet Union's empire
collapses.**

1990-Present
Into a New Century

The end of the Cold War promises a new start.
International co-operation, democracy and peace are
the new hopes.
Many of these hopes are soon dashed.
Communist collapse in Europe breeds uncertainty
and upheaval.
Fear, suspicion and mistrust remain.
New threats emerge. Wars and conflicts start – others
continue.
War still shapes our lives.

As the twentieth century began, Europe continued to dominate world politics and trade. But already, the United States and Japan were emerging as world powers. In 1898, the United States had defeated Spain in a short war, inheriting Spanish colonies in the Far East. Japan had likewise defeated China in the war of 1894-1895. Forming an alliance with Britain in 1902, Japan defeated Russia two years later. In 1900 the United States and Japan joined the European powers in crushing the 'anti-foreigner' uprising in China, a rare example of collaboration between the powers.

At the same time, Britain was at war in South Africa with the Boers. At first, the war went badly for Britain, with its troops suffering a series of defeats. A change in strategy and overwhelming numbers finally broke the Boers and peace was concluded in May 1902. Support for the Boers, especially in Germany, had demonstrated Britain's diplomatic isolation. The war had also shown how little Britain's naval supremacy counted when confronted with a land war.

Even that naval supremacy was challenged when Germany began building a fleet to rival the Royal Navy. Partly because of this, Britain began to emerge from her 'splendid isolation'. The alliance with Japan was followed in 1904 by an understanding with France. A similar arrangement was concluded with Russia in 1907. A fear of Germany, herself allied to Austria-Hungary and Italy, lay at the heart of this Triple Entente. European peace, already endangered by rival alliances, hung by a thread.

left **British Royal Navy Dreadnought battleship. The Dreadnoughts were a new class of heavy battleship built by Britain and Germany. The building programme led to a naval arms race between both countries.**

below **Archduke Franz Ferdinand, heir to the throne of Austria-Hungary, and his wife in Sarajevo, Bosnia, hours before he was assassinated on 28 June 1914 by Gavrilo Princip, a Bosnian Serb nationalist. His death sparked a chain of events that led to the outbreak of the First World War.**

opposite page **Canadian soldiers from C Company of the Royal Canadian Regiment during the Boer War in South Africa.**

The assassination of Archduke Franz Ferdinand, heir to the Austro-Hungarian throne, in Sarajevo on 28 June 1914, provided the spark that ignited the First World War. What started as a quarrel between Austria-Hungary and Serbia became a world war that claimed the lives of 21 million people.

In the West, Germany hoped to defeat France before Russia could fully mobilise. But the French, aided by the British Expeditionary Force, defeated this plan, and by late 1914 both sides were locked in trench warfare. The Western Front became characterised by artillery duels and trench raids, punctuated by offensives costing thousands of lives.

The Eastern Front was more mobile but equally costly. A Russian invasion of Eastern Germany was defeated at Tannenberg in August 1914 and Russia was forced onto the defensive. Huge casualties, food shortages and poor leadership led to the Tsar's overthrow and the establishment of the world's first communist regime in 1917.

Campaigns were also fought in the Balkans, Africa, Italy, the Middle East and Asia. An attempt in 1915 to knock Germany's ally Turkey out of the war was defeated at Gallipoli but they were eventually beaten in Mesopotamia and Palestine.

At sea, the only major battle, was at Jutland in May 1916. It proved indecisive. Britain kept its naval supremacy, despite the German submarine threat. The war produced great strides in aviation. First used for reconnaissance, aircraft were soon employed as fighters and bombers. For the first time, airships - and later aeroplanes - were used to attack civilians.

In March 1918 Germany made an all-out effort to defeat the Allies on the Western Front before the Americans, who entered the war in April 1917, arrived in strength. Initially successful, the Germans were forced back, and by autumn their armies were in full retreat. Germany was forced to sue for an armistice which was signed on 11 November 1918.

left **Army biscuits could be so hard that soldiers often had to mix them with hot water to form a pudding before they could be eaten.**

opposite page **British stretcher-bearers wade through mud on the Western Front on 1 August 1917. The flat ground and high water table in Belgium and Northern France meant that trenches often filled with water and the front line became a muddy quagmire, even in summer.**

'We live in a world where everyone is living solely to kill his fellow man' Lieutenant William St Leger, 2nd Battalion, Coldstream Guards, 19 May 1917

opposite page **German troops mount an attack during their last major offensive in March 1918. The German High Command hoped to break the Allied line and win the war, but the offensive failed.**

right **J W Bakshii was one of two Indian pilots who served in the Royal Flying Corps on the Western Front during the First World War.**

below **People working in a munitions factory in Nottinghamshire, England. Women were encouraged to undertake work that previously only men had been allowed to do. Hundreds of thousands of women volunteered to work in factories, on the land and in offices to help the war effort.**

1919-1939

The Treaty of Versailles, signed on 28 June 1919, formally ended the war. Germany was forced to accept full blame for the conflict and was stripped of territory and its colonies. It was made to pay reparations and the size of its armed forces was severely limited. The Treaty also established the League of Nations, intended to preserve peace and settle international disputes. The end of the war saw the break-up of the German, Austro-Hungarian, Russian and Turkish empires.

After a period of turmoil, the mid-1920s saw the world in a state of apparent stability. This was shattered by the 1929 Wall Street Crash and the subsequent economic depression. In countries severely affected by the Depression, people turned to extremist political movements. Already, in 1922 Mussolini, leader of the Italian fascists, had taken power. In 1933 Hitler became dictator of Germany, tearing up the Versailles Treaty, ruthlessly eliminating political opponents and persecuting Jews.

From 1931 the world began to slide towards another world war. In the Far East, Japan pursued an aggressive foreign policy, invading Manchuria and then setting about the conquest of China. In Europe, Hitler and Mussolini also set their countries on the path of conquest. By 1939 Abyssinia, Albania, Austria and Czechoslovakia had all lost their independence, and in Spain's bloody civil war both dictators supported General Franco. Britain and France had attempted to appease the dictators, but by the summer of 1939 it was clear that war was inevitable.

left **The 'Nuremberg Laws' were introduced by the Nazis in Germany in September 1935. They stripped Jews of their German citizenship, banned them from holding public office and outlawed marriage and sex between Jews and non-Jews.**

opposite page above **Chinese civilians flee from a burning town following Japan's invasion of China in 1937.**

opposite page below **Adolf Hitler addresses a Nazi Party rally at Nuremberg in September 1934. Hitler became Chancellor of Germany in January 1933. Within six months he had established a dictatorship and set up the first of many concentration camps for political opponents.**

1939-1945

On 1 September 1939 Germany invaded Poland. The Second World War had begun. For the first two years there was an unbroken run of German victories. First Poland, then Denmark, Norway, Luxembourg, Holland, Belgium and France were all conquered. In 1941, Yugoslavia and Greece fell to the Germans. Only Britain stood between the Nazis and victory. Having won the Battle of Britain, survived the Blitz, and with the promise of American aid, Britain fought alone until joined by two powerful allies.

The Soviet Union, was invaded by Hitler on 22 June 1941. Initially, German forces were victorious, but suffered their first land defeat at Moscow in December. On 7 December, Japan attacked America at Pearl Harbor. The conflict was now global.

Using the cover of war, Hitler set about the systematic murder of Europe's Jews; six million perished in the Holocaust. Millions of others also died as a result of Nazi policies.

The first half of 1942 saw Germany and Japan triumphant. South East Asia came under Japanese domination, while German advances threatened the Suez Canal and Stalingrad. But in the second half of the year American troops landed on Guadalcanal, the British were victorious at Alamein, and the Russians successfully counter-attacked at Stalingrad.

Allied successes continued throughout 1943 and 1944. The Americans advanced in their Pacific campaign towards Japan. On D-Day, 6 June 1944, the Allies landed in Normandy, beginning the liberation of Western Europe. At the same time, the Russians advanced in the East.

In late 1944, the Allies suffered setbacks at Arnhem and in the Ardennes. But these were temporary, and by spring 1945 the Allies were fighting in Germany. On 30 April, Hitler committed suicide, and a week later Germany surrendered. On 14 August, after atomic bombs were dropped on Hiroshima and Nagasaki, Japan also surrendered.

above **Firemen douse a burning building after German air attacks on Manchester. 593 people were killed in 29 air attacks on the city between 1940 and 1944.**

left **British women welders in the Second World War. In December 1941 women were conscripted into factories because of growing labour shortages. By mid 1944 about 2.5 million women were working in industries making guns, ships, bombers and explosives.**

left British troops come ashore at Normandy during the D-Day landings on 6 June 1944. By the end of the day over 180,000 Allied troops had landed.

below Lancaster bombers were built by Metropolitan Vickers in Trafford Park during the Second World War. The Lancaster was the most successful British bomber of the war.

bottom American troops in action against Japanese forces on Saipan in June 1944.

'We are marked for murder,
all of us'

Israel Makower died Lodz Ghetto, occupied Poland, 1940

24\Timeline
1946-1990

The United States and the Soviet Union emerged from the Second World War as 'superpowers'. Britain was virtually bankrupted by her war effort and Germany was divided. Tensions between the two superpowers developed into the Cold War. An 'Iron Curtain' separated the western democracies and the Soviet Union dominated Eastern Europe. The Berlin Blockade of 1948-1949 hastened the creation of the North Atlantic Treaty Organisation in the West and the Warsaw Pact in the East. In 1961, another crisis over Berlin led to the communist East German government building the Berlin Wall.

Tensions between the superpowers fluctuated during the Cold War. America and Russia battled for influence and control in Africa, Asia and Latin America. Although they never directly came to blows, they fought each other indirectly in Korea, Vietnam, Angola and Afghanistan. Other wars also broke out. Israel fought four wars with its Arab neighbours, while Iran and Iraq fought a bloody conflict between 1980 and 1988. In 1982, Britain and Argentina went to war over the Falkland Islands.

The Cold War saw a nuclear arms race between the United States and the Soviet Union. In October 1962, the siting of Soviet missiles in communist Cuba led to a crisis which brought the world to the brink of nuclear war. The Cuban Missile Crisis had a sobering effect on both superpowers. The relationship between them seemed to improve, especially during the 1970s, a period known as Détente. But in the 1980s relations between the West and the Soviet Union deteriorated again.

The emergence of Mikhail Gorbachev as Soviet leader, and his policies of *Glasnost* and *Perestroika*, began a process which eventually led to the break-up of the Soviet Union and the collapse of its empire in Eastern Europe. In November 1989 the Berlin Wall, symbol of the Cold War in Europe, was torn down by East and West Berliners.

above **A blindfolded Egyptian prisoner of war held captive after the 1973 Yom Kippur War. Syrian and Egyptian forces attacked Israel on the Jewish Holy Day but were defeated after an 18-day battle.**

left **An injured Canadian serviceman is led away from the front during the Korean War. Canadian forces served alongside British, Indian, New Zealand and South African forces in Korea.**

left **The construction of the Berlin Wall begins in August 1961.**

below left **A United States soldier in the Vietnam War. Over one million Vietnamese and 58,000 Americans died during the war.**

below right **West Berlin children watch as an American transport aircraft flies in supplies to the besieged city during the Berlin Airlift of 1948-49. The Soviet Union had blockaded land and rail routes into the western half of the city.**

1990 to Present

The end of the Cold War did not bring about an end to conflict. In 1990 Saddam Hussein, leader of Iraq, invaded Kuwait. An allied coalition ejected the invaders, but failed to topple Saddam Hussein from power. In the former Yugoslavia, politicians fanned ethnic hatreds, seemingly smothered by the old communist regime, and the country erupted again into a series of vicious conflicts. In 1994, genocide occurred in Rwanda where an estimated 800,000 people were murdered amid scenes of appalling brutality.

The United Nations continued to have an important role in peace-keeping operations throughout the world, with British and Commonwealth forces taking a prominent role. Nearer to home, the signing of the Good Friday Agreement in 1998 offered the possibility of an eventual end to the thirty-year conflict in Northern Ireland.

At the beginning of the twenty-first century, terrorism appeared to be the greatest threat to global peace and stability. On 11 September 2001, America and the entire world were stunned when two aircraft hijacked by members of the al Qaeda organisation were flown on suicide missions into the World Trade Center, New York. Another hit the Pentagon in Washington DC and the fourth crashed in Pennsylvania. About 3,000 people died in the attacks. The American response was immediate and determined. President Bush declared an all out 'war on terrorism'. War continues to shape our lives.

left **Kuwaiti children celebrate the liberation of Kuwait City in March 1991. Iraq had invaded Kuwait in August 1990. In January 1991 an international coalition of nations went to war against Iraq to force its army to withdraw from Kuwait.**

below **A Bosnian soldier in the suburb of Dobrinja in Sarajevo in 1992. The war in Bosnia-Herzegovina started in 1992 and lasted until the signing of the Dayton Peace Accords in 1995.**

opposite page **Explosion in the Twin Towers, New York in September 2001. Members of the al Qaeda organisation deliberately flew two hijacked American aeroplanes into the World Trade Center causing both towers to collapse.**

28\Silos

The displays in the towering exhibition spaces within the main gallery focus on themes common to all wars from 1914 to the present. The Silos offer an alternative way of exploring history to the narrative approach of the **Timeline**.

It was challenging to select the initial six themes as there is a huge range of subjects that are central to the history of war and conflict. The exhibition themes vary widely, from people's intensely personal recollections in the **Experience of War** to developments and changes that shape whole societies such as **Science, Technology and War** and the **Legacy of War**. Each Silo illustrates and explores its theme using case studies drawn from both world wars and more recent conflicts. The case studies will change over time to give different perspectives on these themes.

Experience of War

Women and War

Impressions of War

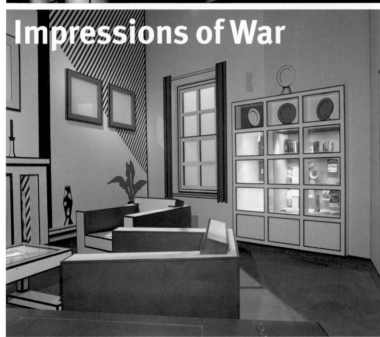

Empire, Commonwealth and War

OUR PROGRESS
...ES IN HARD
WORK

OUR ALLIES
THE
COLONIES

Your Tin makes ENGINE PARTS
for army lorries

Thank you Nigeria !

DO YOU KNO...
IND...

Science, Technology and War

Legacy of War

Liberty and Occupation   Hope

30\Silo
Experience of War

War affects everyone in different ways. This Silo looks at a
selection of common experiences of war: recruitment into
the armed forces, being held as a prisoner of war or internee,
becoming a refugee, and the loss of friends and loved ones.
Using letters, diaries, photographs, objects, artworks and
sound recordings from the archives, the Silo explores the
ways in which these experiences have affected people
caught up in conflicts from the First World War to the
Rwandan genocide.

left **Flying helmet worn by William Baker who was a
talented cartoonist known as Biff. He served as an air
gunner in Bomber Command with No 115 and No 626
Squadrons during the Second World War. On 30 January
1944, his aircraft was badly damaged during a raid on
Berlin and he was knocked unconscious. After regaining
consciousness he operated the rear gun turret by hand
throughout the journey home. He was awarded the
Distinguished Flying Cross for his bravery.**

opposite page **Joseph and Daisy Cooper were married in
West London in July 1918. Joseph had served with the
2/20th Battalion, The London Regiment in Palestine and
Salonika, Greece from 1916 before being transferred to
the Western Front. He survived the war.**

32\Silo
Women and War

The role of women as carers of the sick and wounded is well known, but their other war work is sometimes overlooked. This exhibition focuses on the range of jobs that women carried out during both world wars, many previously the preserve of men. Women talk about what it was like to make munitions during the First World War, work as Land Girls and as reporters in the front line in the 1940s. Other women from around the world discuss their contrasting experiences of going into combat or protesting against war. The exhibition shows how women have contributed to war in so many different ways and how it has affected their lives.

below left **Flora Sandes was the only British woman to fight as a soldier in the First World War. She enlisted with the Serbian army during their retreat to Kosovo in 1915. Flora rose through the ranks to become a sergeant major. She was seriously wounded in 1916 and was later awarded the Serbian Order of Karageorge for her bravery.**

below right **Emma Kay worked as a humanitarian aid worker in Bosnia-Herzegovina during the war in the former Yugoslav republic. In 1998 Emma joined the International Medical Corps in Kosovo where she helped to set up mobile clinics. She was forced to leave Kosovo in 1999 but continued her aid work in refugee camps in Albania and Macedonia during the NATO air war.**

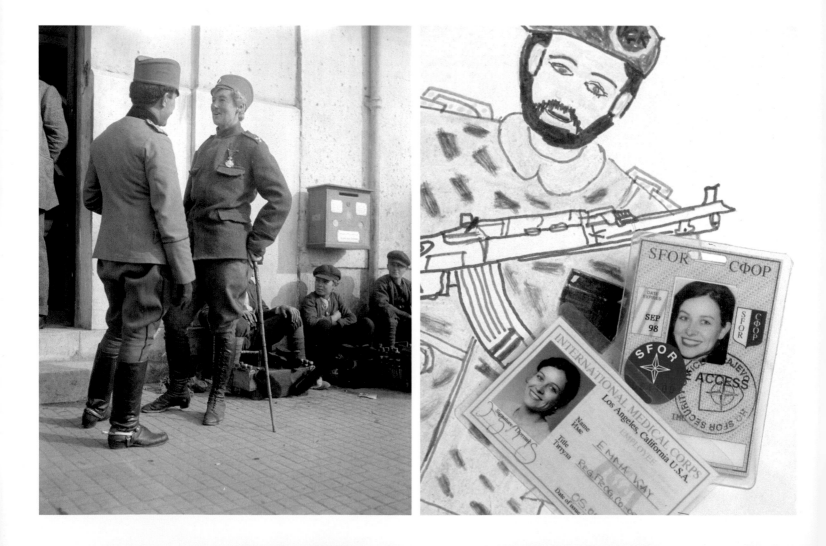

Born in Liverpool, Lilian Bader worked as an Aircraft Instrument Repairer with the Women's Auxiliary Air Force during the Second World War.
'I passed out first class... I was always willing to learn because it was such a treat after domestic service to be able to use your brain and do things.'

34\Silo
Impressions of War

We all have an idea of what war is like. Some people have experienced war at first hand. Others have seen live coverage on television or have gained an impression of war by reading books, playing games, or visiting museums. But are our impressions correct? This exhibition explores the many ways that people find out about war, the role of the media, and the use of propaganda. It also tries to distinguish some of the 'facts' from fiction. Case studies look at the factors that have shaped our knowledge of the two world wars and the conflicts in Vietnam and the Falklands. They highlight how we define the 'facts' and how they can change over time.

above **Winston Churchill and Lord Halifax. After the resignation of the Prime Minister Neville Chamberlain in 1940, many believed that Lord Halifax would become Prime Minister, not Winston Churchill.**

left **British Royal Marine Commandos walk the last mile into Port Stanley during the 1982 Falklands War. The British government imposed tight restrictions on the reporting of the war.**

below and opposite page **Cartoon book about the life of Winston Churchill.**

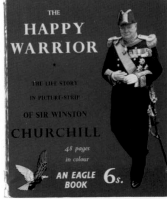

Empire, Commonwealth and War

People from the British Empire and Commonwealth fought alongside Britain during both world wars. Over 300,000 died. They worked to provide vital goods, raw materials and supplies for the war effort. After the Second World War many people in Asia and Africa revolted against British rule, which accelerated the move from Empire to Commonwealth. This exhibition focuses on a selection of experiences from across the British Empire and Commonwealth during both world wars and in the immediate aftermath of the Second World War. It explores the close, complex and changing relationship between the British Empire, the Commonwealth and Britain.

opposite page **1 Unknown Canadian Nursing Sister 2 Ezikel Lopez, forestry worker from British Honduras 3 Able Seaman Ramazani of the Tanganyika Naval Force 4 L D Jafar Khan of the Indian Armoured Corps 5 Private Kisarisha of the East African Pioneers 6 Unknown soldier of the King's African Rifles 7 Lieutenant Colonel C P Jayawardene of the 1st Battalion Ceylon Light Infantry 8 Unknown soldier of the British West Indies Regiment 9 Unknown New Zealand Maori soldier 10 Unknown West Indian members of the Auxiliary Territorial Service 11 Home Guard John Wade from Montserrat 12 Unknown soldier of the Indian Light Armoured Squadron 13 Unknown soldier of the King's African Rifles 14 Unknown sapper sergeant of the Singapore Straights Settlements Volunteers 15 Sergeant J Camilleri of the 11th Heavy Anti-Aircraft Regiment, Royal Malta Artillery 16 Unknown Canadian pilot 17 Mr A J Cox of Buganda and Goswa Kasaja of the African Auxiliary Pioneer Corps 18 RAF crewman Robert Ngbaronye of Nigeria**

left **Flying Officer Gilbert Fairweather was a Royal Air Force navigator from British Honduras (modern day Belize). Gilbert was killed one year after this photo was taken in June 1944 when his plane was shot down over Germany. He was 22 years old.**

below **Indian soldiers fought on the Western Front, Palestine, Gallipoli, Mesopotamia (modern Iraq) and East Africa during the First World War.**

38\Silo
Science, Technology and War

War has sparked and accelerated some of the most important scientific, medical and technical innovations of the twentieth century. Governments have invested heavily to improve their chances of winning wars, increasing their fighting ability and weakening the enemy. Some of these developments, such as poison gas and the atomic bomb, have wreaked devastation. Others in the fields of communications and medical care have had more positive benefits. The jet engine has served a dual purpose. It has advanced the possibilities of aerial warfare but has also made travel between nations easier and faster.

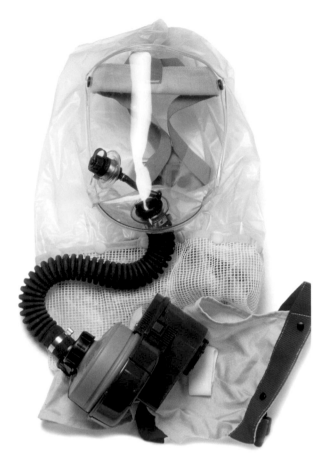

above **Child's gas mask issued to Israeli children in 1990 to protect against the danger of Iraqi chemical attacks on the country before the start of the 1991 Gulf War.**

left **The distinctive mushroom cloud created by the explosion of an atomic bomb rises 20,000 feet above the Japanese city of Nagasaki just after 11.00 am on 9 August 1945. The explosion killed 73,884 people.**

opposite page **An Australian Army gas sentry sounds the alarm in June 1916. Poison gas was widely used by both sides during the First World War.**

'Gas! GAS! Quick, boys! An ecstasy of fumbling,
Fitting the clumsy helmets just in time;
But someone still was yelling out and stumbling,
And flound'ring like a man in fire or lime...
Dim, through the misty panes and thick green light,
As under a green sea, I saw him drowning.

In all my dreams, before my helpless sight,
He plunges at me, guttering, choking, drowning.'

Wilfred Owen 'Dulce Et Decorum Est'

40\Silo
Legacy of War

The impact of war does not end the day the fighting stops. Wars have consequences that last for many generations. Some of these legacies are obvious. People severely injured by war, mentally or physically, may be scarred for life. Devastated towns and cities need to be rebuilt and repaired. Other legacies of war are less obvious but can affect entire nations. Economies can be left ruined whereas others prosper with the return to peace. Societies can also experience profound political and social change after war. People reject pre-war ways of thinking and look for new ideas and solutions for the future. Yet more legacies of war remain hidden. Landmines and unexploded bombs continue to kill and maim years after the fighting has finished.

above **Hetem and Syleme's house and contents were destroyed by NATO cluster bombs during the 1999 Kosovo War. Before the war Mrs Ahmeti had earned an income mending clothes with a sewing machine which was destroyed in the attack. One year after the war ended the Ahmetis were still living in a United Nations refugee tent. They could not rebuild their house because of the danger of unexploded bombs.**

opposite page **1 Minefield warning sign from Angola 2 Syleme Ahmeti's sewing machine 3 Electric American football game 4 Spent bullet cartridges 5 Knuckle duster 6 NATO bomb fragment from Kosovo 7 Stethoscope from an NHS family doctor 8 Cluster bomblet 9 Homemade teddy bear 10 Crushed French water bottle 11 Leftover tins of United Nations emergency food 12 Artificial leg**

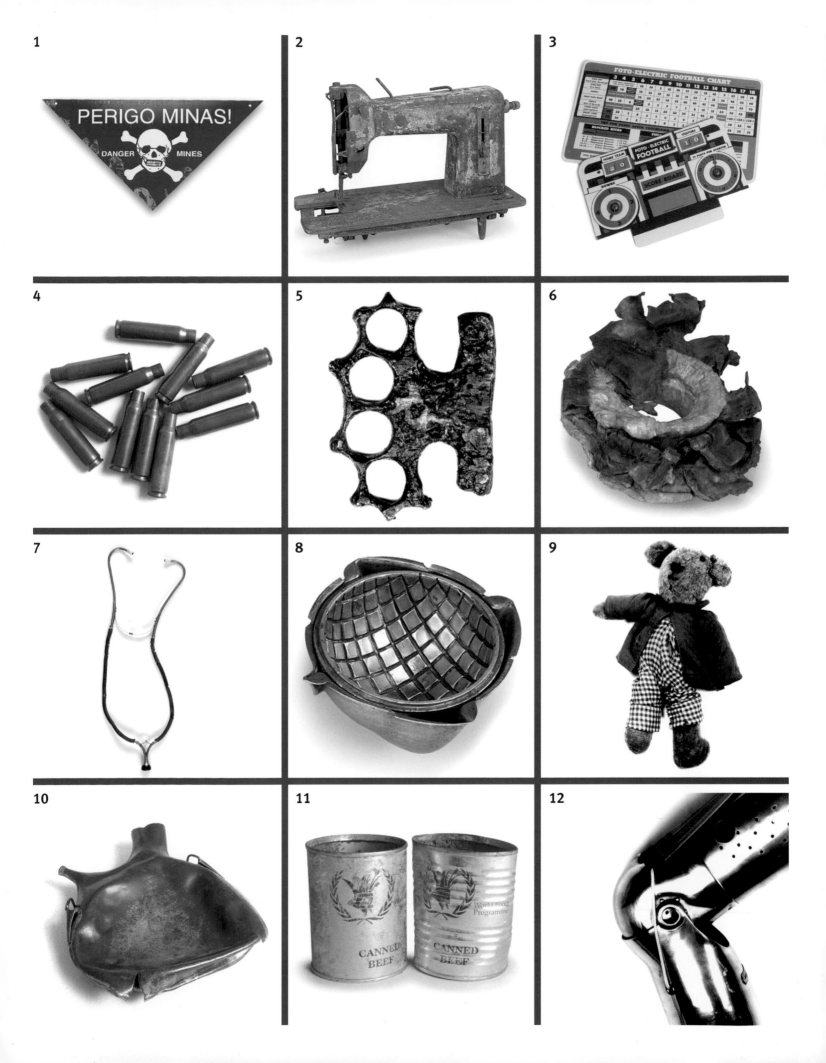

Visitors can call up objects from the Museum's collections in the **TimeStacks**. At the touch of a button trays of objects appear behind glass. The material is grouped into themes including animals in war, gadgets and guides to help escape capture, soldiers' trench art and cameras in conflict. At certain times of the day, Museum staff are on hand so that visitors can touch, handle and discuss objects from the **TimeStacks**.

opposite page **1 Sculpture of Judy the dog 2 German Pickelhaube helmet 3 Army surgical kit 4 Souvenir trench art 5 Engraved shell case 6 Paper knife from Baghdad 7 Queen Alexandra's 1914 gift tin 8 Cloth map 9 Dog's gas mask 10 Saddle pouch 11 Escape and evasion phrase book 12 Trench football game 13 Crucifix made from bullets 14 Unit sign, No.1 Army Auxiliary Horse Company 15 Harness from Rex the dog 16 Magnetized pencil clip 17 Princess Mary's gift fund box 18 Swagger stick 19 Ammunition box 20 Escape and evasion miniature saw**

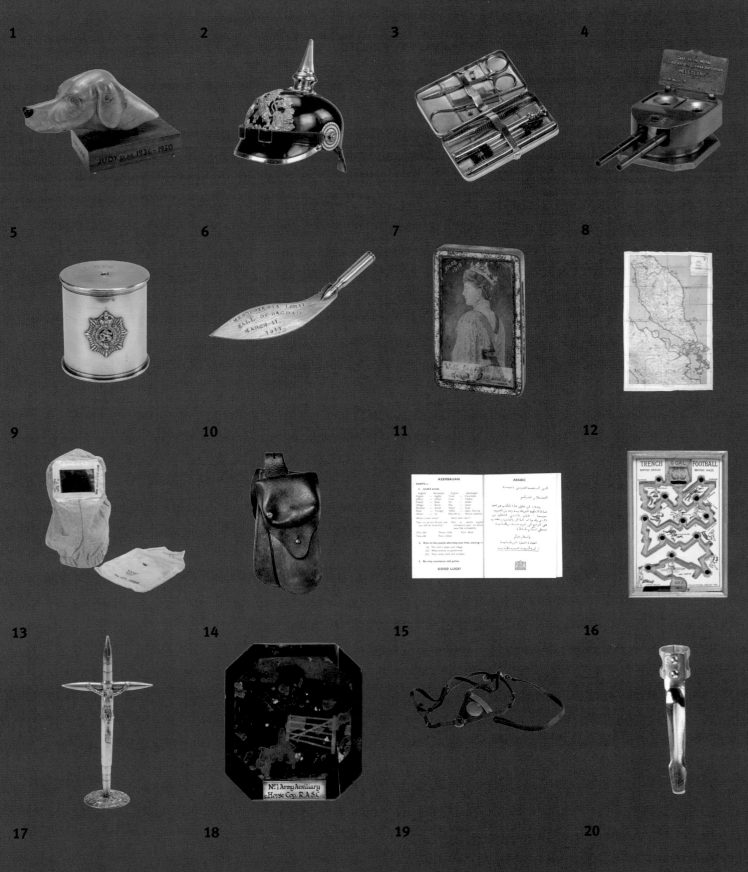

44\Daniel Libeskind and Imperial War Museum North

Daniel Libeskind is an international figure in architectural design, well known for his expressive and inventive buildings. He won the commission for Imperial War Museum North in June 1997 and this is his first building in the UK.

The building is intriguing. The three interlocking shards have their own distinct shape, creating unique spaces. Visitors enter through the Air Shard which pierces the building like a piece of shrapnel. It stands 55 metres high and is neither exterior nor interior but a transitional space, preparing people for their visit. The Earth Shard is perhaps the most surprising space of all. Here visitors can experience the curvature of the earth in the Main Exhibition Space and Special Exhibitions Gallery. The Water Shard slopes gracefully towards the Manchester Ship Canal and is home to the Museum Restaurant.

Construction started in January 2000, using a limited range of materials in an inventive way – concrete, steelwork, render and aluminium cladding. The design presented a variety of construction challenges. As the Works Manager once said, 'If it looks right you know it's wrong and if it looks wrong you know it's right!' In the Air Shard, which contains no less than 230 tonnes of steelwork, the concrete stair core looks as if it is leaning. In fact, it is upright and it is the Air Shard which is four degrees from the vertical.

The building features simple but innovative technical solutions, ranging from an environmentally-friendly cooling system that channels canal water through pipes embedded in the floor to the use of fluorescent lights which represent slashes of light in the sky.

Libeskind has not only created a brilliant building, he has worked closely with the project and design teams to create an extraordinary museum. As he says, 'What makes Imperial War Museum North unique is the integration of architecture, exhibition design, engineering and a vision of history and the future'.

'Conflict has been a constant factor of the twentieth century as the world has repeatedly fragmented into warring factions. I have imagined the globe broken into fragments and taken the pieces to form the building – three shards – together they represent conflict on land, in the air and on water.'

Daniel Libeskind

opposite The dramatic 55 metre Air Shard rises above the Water Shard. The Restaurant inside the Water Shard has views over the Manchester Ship Canal .

left The 29 metre high viewing platform inside the Air Shard offers spectacular views of the city of Manchester.

below The Main Exhibition Space is in the Earth Shard, where the floor is shaped to reflect the curvature of the earth and the jagged, recessed lighting is designed to cut across the path of the sun as it moves over the building. The Air Shard is designed to be seen from a distance, announcing the presence of the Museum.

48\Further Information

Special Exhibitions
The Special Exhibitions Gallery (below) hosts a changing programme of exciting and stimulating exhibitions.

Learning
The Museum is a lifelong learning resource which is flexible, varied and focuses on the power of the objects. People of all ages can explore the themes and collections in more depth in the Learning Studio. Call us to discuss your needs on 0161 836 4064.

Visitor Services
The Museum has a cloakroom, toilets, baby changing facilities, Museum Shop and Café on the ground floor, and a magnificent restaurant with views over the Manchester Ship Canal on the gallery level. There is wheelchair access into and through all Museum galleries.

Mailing List
Keep in touch by joining our mailing list. For more information please call us on 0161 836 4000.

Corporate Hire
The Museum offers a spectacular setting for formal dinners, drinks receptions, presentations and product launches. The Main Exhibition Space, Special Exhibitions Gallery, Restaurant and Red Room are all available for hire. For more details please contact us on 0161 836 4042.

Get involved
To find out how you can get involved as a Friend of Imperial War Museum North or by becoming a volunteer, please call 0161 836 4000. If you would like to give a donation or legacy to the Museum, or to discover more about business sponsorship, please call our Development Team on 0161 836 4031.